A 40-DAY GUIDE FOR SEEKING GOD

SEEKING A *familiar* FACE

THE
COMPANION
WORKBOOK TO
*SEEKING A
FAMILIAR FACE: THE
TRANSFORMATIONAL
JOURNEY OF
CONNECTING
WITH GOD*

BY MAY PATTERSON

Contents

Introduction

Ever feel distant from God? Do you long to grow nearer to Him, but yet sometimes you just can't seem to get there? If you have ever struggled to find time to connect with God or if you tend to get sidetracked, then this study is for you. For forty days it will guide you through the stories of biblical characters who often felt the same way. This study will lead you to spend time with God, and as you discover more about Him, you will also discover a lot about yourself.

I wrote *Seeking a Familiar Face* and this companion workbook, *A 40-Day Guide for Seeking God*, to encourage you to seek after the Lord as a daily practice. Nothing can change your life more. Spending time with God nourishes our souls—a part of us that we often neglect. In His presence we find soul-rest. Transformation. Peace. And the power to live and to love like we never could on our own.

God promises:

"When you call on me, when you come and pray to me, I'll listen. When you come looking for me, you'll find me. Yes, when you get serious about finding me and want it more than anything else, I'll make sure you won't be disappointed."
Jer. 29:12-14 MSG

Years ago, I felt distant from God. I attended church and tried to be a good person, but I didn't take spending time with Him very seriously. God was busy in heaven; I was busy on earth. Our paths just didn't seem to cross much. I was an occasional seeker—at best—focusing more on being religious than on building a relationship. As a result, I felt far away from God and pretty weak and empty inside.

So when my life became more demanding, I buckled.

I had *three* children in *two* years. The responsibility for so many little lives felt way too heavy because I was so focused on my own life. Postpartum depression set in. "I can't" became my motto. Finally, in desperation I began to reach out for God every day. At first, it seemed like I didn't make much of a connection. But I kept on trying, hoping He would help me.

Like the verse above promises, I was not (and am not) disappointed. At the busiest time of my life, I found a source of rest. I found the love and strength I so desperately needed. When I got *serious* about seeking the Lord (as a practice), my entire life changed. The more time I spent in His presence, the more I began to feel a sense of purpose, strength and joy.

Now I really don't resemble the unhappy person I was back then (thank goodness).

If this happened for me, it can happen for you.

I want you to find the same blessings that I've found. Forty days of seeking God in an intentional, focused way will change your heart and eventually, change your life— **it's impossible for it not to**. Years from now, you will look back on this time and be grateful, for no time spent with God is ever wasted.

Commit to walking close to the Lord's side for the next forty days, using this guide. Read His word. Answer the daily questions. Journal. Practice the meditations. Build your relationship with God. You will not be the same on day forty-one!

It doesn't matter if you have been seeking God for years or are just beginning, this guide will help you draw nearer than ever before, leading you closer to Him, one encounter at a time.

HOW TO USE THIS BOOK

I designed this *40-Day Guide for Seeking God* to pair with my book, *Seeking a Familiar Face*. If you don't have the book yet, I hope you will get one, along with a journal and a Bible, and get started on the journey.

During the next forty days, we will dig deeper into the stories of the ten biblical characters who are featured in *Seeking a Familiar Face*. This guide provides thought-provoking questions and plenty of writing space for each day. I've even added an extra discussion and journaling page titled "What Do You Think?" to each chapter, to encourage you to think, write and talk about what God reveals to you during the forty days.

Of course, there is no one "right" way to seek the Lord, but this guide will help you. It will encourage you to read the Bible and to apply its principles to everyday life. It will lead you to write out your prayers and to meditate. I'm so excited about the great things you will discover!

But along with the benefits of seeking God, I must also give you fair warning: on some days seeking God may be difficult. It may feel like you aren't making a connection. Possibly, it might seem like you're wasting your time. You may experience opposition. Multiple distractions will probably arise.

Don't quit. Commit to seek God for forty days—even if it's hard—and He will reward you (Heb. 11:6).

And for those crazy days when seeking God seems impossible, I've added a section of two-to-four-minute meditations to the end of this book. If you can't sit down, read and answer the questions, then simply meditate. I'll guide you.

Meditation is simply a focused pause—a few minutes of gazing up at God, instead of fixating on problems and "to do" lists. Sounds pretty good, doesn't it? In fact, you may enjoy these meditations so much that you keep on practicing them long after the forty days are over.

MY PRAYER FOR YOU

As you embark on this forty-day journey of seeking the Lord, I'm praying that you will find:
- Deeper connection with Him.
- Soul-rest and renewal.
- Encouragement for every trial you're facing.
- A transformed heart and life.
- A new sense of purpose and fulfillment.
- Hope and guidance for the future.

Are you ready? Let's start seeking the Lord together today!

Josiah

"SEEKING GOD HAS A RIPPLE EFFECT FROM
HERE TO ETERNITY, TOUCHING INDIVIDUALS,
LIVES AND CIRCUMSTANCES MORE THAN WE
MAY EVER KNOW."

SEEKING A FAMILIAR FACE, PAGE 26

JOSIAH: DAY 1

Come On, Let's Go!

Meditate on the following verses:

"When you call on me, when you come and pray to me, I'll listen. When you come looking for me, you'll find me. Yes, when you get serious about finding me and want it more than anything else, I'll make sure you won't be disappointed . . ."

Jer. 29:12-14 MSG

1. Are you seeking God on a regular basis right now? If you're struggling to find time to spend with God, you are not alone! List obstacles that might prevent you from seeking God in the space below. Pray over this list, asking God to help you overcome anything that might stand in your way.

2. God asks us to seek Him over fifty times in the Bible because it's not something we do naturally—seeking God is a *learned* practice. And a powerful one! Write a prayer asking God to help you commit to 40 days of seeking Him through this guide. Sign and date it.

3. You don't have to seek the Lord alone! Find a friend (or two) to seek along with you as you work through this guide. Seeking together will encourage you, bringing you closer to God and to your friend(s). List the names of people who might join you. Pray over the list and then ask someone (or several) to join you for 40 days of seeking God.

Answer God's Call

Read 2 Kings 22-23 along with "Josiah Seeks" in
Seeking a Familiar Face, **pages 20-22.**

1. What may have motivated Josiah, who lived in a very wicked and idolatrous time, to seek after God?

2. What difficult mission did God call Josiah to do? What reforms did he make?

3. What difficult thing has or is God calling you to do? How does Josiah's story encourage you? What do you learn from his sincerity and obedience?

Consider the Ripple Effect

1. Read about King Josiah in 2 Chron. 34-35. When Josiah was sixteen years old, he decided to seek after the Lord. Who was affected by Josiah's decision? List as many individuals and groups as you can. (Hint: consider the ripple effect of his decision over time.)

2. Josiah's story teaches us that our seeking God affects other people, too. List the names of individuals and groups who might be affected by your seeking as you work through this guide. Pray over this list, asking God to make you a blessing to each one.

3. How did seeking the Lord change Josiah's life? List the things God called him to do. How might seeking God change your life? What might God call you to do?

Let Go of Guilt

Consider what the following verse means to you today:

"Because your heart was responsive, and you humbled yourself before God when you heard what he spoke against this place and its people, and because you humbled yourself before me and tore your robes and wept in my presence, I have heard you, declares the Lord."

2 Chron. 34:27

1. Read 2 Chron. 34:14-33. Before Josiah was born, the Law (the first five books of the Old Testament) had been lost. It was found while the temple was being restored. When Josiah first heard the word of God, he was guilt-stricken. Have you ever felt that way? How did you respond?

2. List words that describe Josiah's response from verses 27-33.

3. How did God respond to Josiah? (see verses 27-28) What does this teach you about God's response to heartfelt repentance? (See Ps. 51:17)

4. Is there something you need to repent of today? As you seek God, ask Him to reveal your sin. Repent of whatever He brings to mind. Write about it below. Repentance removes the barrier of sin and draws us closer to God.

1. Journal about how your completing this 40-day seeking guide could possibly affect someone close to you. Discuss your thoughts about the ripple effect of seeking God with a friend.

2. Find three verses about seeking God in the Bible. Paraphrase these Scriptures in a journal using personal pronouns, as if these verses were written just to you. Beside each verse, write down anything you feel God is saying to you.

3. Journal about how the *practice* of seeking God might draw you closer to Him as you work through this 40-day guide.

4. Journal about what impacted you most as you sought God through this chapter.

5. Share the main points you are taking away from this chapter with a friend.

Moses

"LIKE MOSES, WE GET TO SEE BRIEF GLIMPSES OF
GOD TO STRENGTHEN AND HELP US WHILE WE
ARE STILL FAR AWAY FROM OUR FUTURE HOME.
THESE GLIMPSES CONFIRM WHERE WE ARE GOING.
THEY CAN PULL US OUT OF THE PIT OF DESPAIR.
EACH TIME WE SEEK GOD'S GLORY, IT ENABLES US
TO WALK ON WITH RESOLVE, CONTINUING OUR
JOURNEY TOWARD ETERNITY WITH HIM."

SEEKING A FAMILIAR FACE, PAGE 42

Overcome Failure & Loss

Read about Moses in Exod. 33:18-23 and 34:5-7, along with "Moses Seeks"
in *Seeking a Familiar Face*, pages 32-33.

"If then you have been raised with Christ, seek the things that are above, where Christ
is, seated at the right hand of God. Set your minds on things that are above, not on
things that are on earth."
Col. 3:1-2 ESV

Seeking for the "things that are above" means seeking God's greatness or glory:
who He is, what He has done, and what He will do in the future. **Focusing on God's**
glory dramatically changes our perspective. It gives our minds a needed break,
especially if we've failed, suffered loss, or feel depressed.

1. Read Exod. 2:11-15. How did Moses fail as an Egyptian Prince?
   Read Acts 7:38-39. How did Moses fail as a leader?
   How have you failed lately?

2. Moses responded to failure, loss and disappointment by praying, "Show me your glory."
   It was his prayer for despair. What do you learn from this unusual prayer?

3. How could seeking God's glory help you overcome past failures?

Look Up in Awe

Meditate on the following verses:

"The heavens proclaim the glory of God. The skies display his craftsmanship. Day after day they continue to speak; night after night they make him known. They speak without a sound or word; their voice is never heard. Yet their message has gone throughout the earth, and their words to all the world." Ps. 19:1-4 NLT

Seek God's glory today by exploring *who He is.*

1. Read Ps. 19. From this passage (and others), make a list of God's character traits, such as Creator, trustworthy, etc. What hope does this list give you today?

2. How have you benefited personally from one of God's character traits?

3. Make a list of words and phrases that describe God's glory in Exod. 34:6-7. Do you use this kind of language when you talk about God or pray to Him? How could you incorporate more words of glory, praise, and awe into the way you think and talk?

Remember Your Rescue

Meditate on the following verses:

". . . the Lord rescued you with such a strong hand from your slavery and from the oppressive hand of Pharaoh, king of Egypt. Understand, therefore, that the Lord your God is indeed God. He is the faithful God who keeps his covenant for a thousand generations and lavishes his unfailing love on those who love him and obey his commands." Deut. 7:8-9 NLT

Seek God's glory today by remembering *what He has done for you*: the promises He has kept and the provision He has made.

1. Read Exod. 12:31-42. How did God fulfill His promise to rescue the Israelites from Egypt? How did He provide for them?

2. How has God rescued you in the past? How has He provided for you?

3. Read Col. 1:13-14. How is the rescue of the Israelites from Egyptian bondage similar to our rescue from the bondage of sin?

Consider Your Glorious Future

Meditate on the following verses:

"But let me reveal to you a wonderful secret. We will not all die, but we will all be transformed! It will happen in a moment, in the blink of an eye, when the last trumpet is blown. For when the trumpet sounds, those who have died will be raised to live forever. And we who are living will also be transformed." 1 Cor. 15:51-52 NLT

Seek God's glory today by focusing on *what He will do* for you in the future.

1. Read Rev. 22:1-6. What might meeting the Lord be like? What sights, sounds, smells and emotions might you experience? How does attempting to picture this moment build your faith?

2. Read Rev. 21-22. List some of the wonderful benefits of heaven and eternity with the Lord. What do these future blessings mean to you in light of your current circumstances?

3. Does considering your future inheritance bring you hope? Write out a concise statement describing the hope you have as a believer in Christ. Who could you share this with today?

What Do You Think?

1. How did Moses respond after his encounter with God's glory? (See Exod. 34:8) Journal about a time when you encountered God's glory. How did you respond?

2. After seeking God's glory in this guide, how has your understanding of it changed? How does His glory lift you up?

3. Journal about one of God's character traits. How has this trait impacted your life? What hope does it give you for your life today? Share your thoughts with a friend.

4. Moses's face was radiant after his encounter with God (Exod. 34:29-35). God's shining glory transferred to Moses, literally. How does (or will) spending time with God affect your countenance and emotions?

5. What impacted you most about this chapter? Share one thing you are taking away from this chapter with a friend.

The Thief

"Meditating on what Christ did for us enables grace to shape our lives and our futures in a powerful way. It gives us amazing strength to love and serve others. If we let grace flow through us, it will come back around and bless us further."

Seeking a Familiar Face, pages 56- 57

THE THIEF: DAY 1

A Change of Heart

Read about the thieves at the Crucifixion in Matt. 27:38-44 and Luke 23:32-43, along with "A Thief Seeks" in *Seeking a Familiar Face*, pages 48-49.

1. Matthew and Luke give different accounts of the thieves at the Crucifixion. Apparently, one of them had a change of heart toward Jesus after hanging next to Him. Why do you think Jesus was crucified between one who believed and one who did not? How do the attitudes of the thieves differ?

2. According to Luke 23:40-43, how did the thief confess his sin? How did he reveal his change of heart?

3. What do you need to repent of today? Write a prayer below, confessing your sin and asking the Lord to change your heart.

God's Grace Is for You

Like the thief, we are all sinners in need of grace. Picture yourself in the thief's place, as a condemned, dying person who finds salvation in Christ. The verses below are paraphrased with personal pronouns. Read them out loud, as if they were written just to you:

*"I was made right with God by placing my faith in Jesus Christ.
And this is true for anyone who believes, even me, no matter who I am.
For I have sinned; I've fallen short of God's glorious standard.
Yet God freely and graciously declares that I am righteous. He did this through
Christ Jesus when he freed me from the penalty for my sins."
Rom. 3:22-24 NLT (paraphrased)*

*"Because of my faith, Christ has brought me into this place of undeserved privilege
where I now stand, and I confidently and joyfully look forward to sharing God's glory."
Rom. 5:2 NLT (paraphrased)*

*"If I declare with my mouth, 'Jesus is Lord,' and believe in my heart that God raised him from
the dead, I will be saved. For it is with my heart that I believe and am justified,
and it is with my mouth that I profess my faith and am saved.
As Scripture says, 'Anyone who believes in him will never be put to shame.'"
Rom. 10: 9-11 NIV (paraphrased)*

1. Which words or phrases are the most meaningful to you today? Which truths are you grateful for? Why?

2. In light of your current problems, which phrases bring you comfort? Why?

THE THIEF: DAY 3

Receive the Gift of Grace

As we seek to grasp the meaning of the gospel, we will find the Lord nearby.

1. Write the gospel in your own words. Base it on Scripture and list references. Make it concise, understandable, and conversational in form.

2. Do you find it hard to receive salvation as a gift? Read the following verses and list reasons why salvation is not earned.

   "But God is so rich in mercy, and he loved us so much, that even though we were dead because of our sins, he gave us life when he raised Christ from the dead . . . God saved you by his grace when you believed. And you can't take credit for this; it is a gift from God. Salvation is not a reward for the good things we have done, so none of us can boast about it."
   Eph. 2:4-5, 8-9 NLT

3. What things do people try to add to the finished work of salvation? Are you attempting to add anything?

Let Grace Overflow

1. Read John 1:14-18 and write a prayer thanking God for the gift of grace. Include specific reasons why you are grateful and ask God to help you extend grace to others.

2. Humility enables us to both receive and extend grace (1 Pet. 5:5). Look at the examples in the "Pride and Humility" chart on page 54 in *Seeking a Familiar Face*. Which example challenges you today? Why? Which example would you most like to adopt?

3. List the names of people to whom you can extend grace today. Beside each name write how you can give grace to him or her, specifically. Pray over the list.

THE THIEF

1. How can we mirror the gospel story in everyday life? What traits, attitudes and actions reflect grace?

2. What actions and attitudes might hide the gospel from someone? Have you ever "hidden" the gospel? Journal about what you learned and discuss it with a friend.

3. What blessings does God promise to believers? Name as many as you can. Journal about what these blessings mean to you. Share your thoughts with a friend.

4. Journal about three specific ways you can accept God's grace this week.

5. Journal about three specific ways you can extend grace to others this week.

Mary of Bethany

"WE NEED TO KNOW WE ARE LOVED.
EVERY. SINGLE. DAY."

SEEKING A FAMILIAR FACE, PAGE 71

MARY OF BETHANY: DAY 1

Experience the Love of God

Read Luke 10:38-42, Mark 14:3-9 and John 12:1-7 along with "Mary of Bethany Seeks" in *Seeking a Familiar Face*, pages 63-65.

1. What decisions did Mary make in order to seek after Jesus? What did she receive from Him? What decisions (to seek) will you make today? What might you receive?

2. Read Eph. 3:18-19. In this passage, Paul prays for believers to experience God's love, even though we can never fully grasp it. Why is this important? How could you experience God's love this week?

3. How did Mary love Jesus in return? List ways you can love the Lord today.

   a. In your thoughts:

   b. In your words:

   c. In your actions:

Open Your Eyes

Meditate on the following verse:

"In the same way, we can see and understand only a little about God now, as if we were peering at his reflection in a poor mirror; but someday we are going to see him in his completeness, face-to-face . . ." 1 Cor. 13:12 TLB

1. List three tangible ways God has displayed His love in your life.

2. Find a picture to remind you of each thing on your list. Attach an appropriate Scripture to each picture. Place these "love pictures" on your bulletin board or fridge as visual reminders of God's love.

3. Transform your day by focusing on the love of the Lord and storing it up in your heart. Meditate on the following verses:

   "Consider the kind of extravagant love the Father has lavished on us—He calls us children of God! It's true; we are His beloved children . . ." 1 John 3:1 VOICE

   "But from everlasting to everlasting the Lord's love is with those who fear him, and his righteousness with their children's children—with those who keep his covenant and remember to obey his precepts." Ps. 103:17-18

   "The steadfast love of the Lord never ceases; his mercies never come to an end; they are new every morning; great is your faithfulness. 'The Lord is my portion,' says my soul, 'therefore I will hope in him.' The Lord is good to those who wait for him, to the soul who seeks him." Lam. 3:22-25 ESV

Proclaim It!

Read the following verses out loud:

"It is good to proclaim your unfailing love in the morning, your faithfulness in the evening." Ps. 92:2 NLT

"Publish his glorious deeds among the nations. Tell everyone about the amazing things he does." Ps. 96:3 NLT

1. How often do you say, "God loves me," out loud? List some of the possible benefits of proclaiming God's love audibly.

2. Satan often deceives believers into thinking that God doesn't love them anymore. Has Satan ever deceived you with this lie? How can speaking truth out loud help you believe God loves you?

3. The Apostle John often referred to himself as "the disciple whom Jesus loved." John felt special because Jesus loved him. Do you? Do you ever refer to yourself this way? If not, why not?

Celebrate Emmanuel

*"I have been crucified with Christ and I no longer live, but Christ lives in me.
The life I now live in the body, I live by faith in the Son of God, who loved me
and gave himself for me." Gal. 2:20*

1. How does Emmanuel, or the Spirit of Christ dwelling within you, bless your life?
    Name as many blessings as you can. (See Eph. 1:13-14, 2 Cor. 1:21-22, Rom. 8:11)

2. Read 1 John 4:11-16. Write a short prayer thanking God for the love He has given you in
    Jesus Christ.

3. God said, *". . . Can a mother forget her nursing child? Can she feel no love for the child
    she has borne? But even if that were possible, I would not forget you! See, I have written
    your name on the palms of my hands." Isa. 49:15-16 NLT*

    What does your name being written on God's hands mean to you? How can you celebrate
    this truth throughout the day?

MARY OF BETHANY

What Do You Think?

· ✳ ·

1. Read Eph. 3:14-19. Why is it important to fill your heart daily with the love of God? Discuss this with a friend.

2. Journal about a time when God displayed His great love for you. How did He work on your behalf? How was He your refuge or shield? Share your experience with a friend.

3. Do you find it difficult to say, "God loves me" out loud? Why or why not? Journal about the benefits of speaking truth out loud and then share them with a friend.

4. Have you ever *felt* Christ's presence within you? If so, journal about it. What comfort does this give you? Ask a friend to share his or her experience with you.

5. 1 John 4:16 NIV says, "*. . . Whoever **lives in love** lives in God, and God in them.*" How can you "live in love" today?

   a. As a parent:

   b. As a spouse:

   c. As a coworker:

   d. As a neighbor:

Zacchaeus

"GOD WANTS TO FREE US TO ENJOY HIM AND
TO ENJOY OUR LIVES. HE CAN SATISFY US
MORE THAN 'HAVING MORE' EVER CAN. WHEN
WE TREASURE OUR TIME WITH HIM
MORE THAN ANYTHING ELSE, THEN WE
BECOME TRULY RICH."

SEEKING A FAMILIAR FACE, PAGE 80

Go Out on a Limb!

Read Luke 19:1-10 along with "Zacchaeus Seeks" in
***Seeking a Familiar Face*, pages 76-78.**

1. Zacchaeus sought the Lord in an undignified way, by climbing a tree. Have you ever gone "out on a limb" in pursuit of the Lord? If so, what happened?

2. How did the Lord respond to Zacchaeus? How did He respond to you?

3. Why does Jesus say that He seeks after *us* in verse 10? How does the idea of being pursued by the Lord encourage you as you seek Him? How does it challenge you?

Break Free from Bondage

1. List possible reasons why Zacchaeus valued money more than he valued the Lord.

2. Take a look at your calendar and checkbook; what do they indicate that you value? How did Zacchaeus break away from the bondage of valuing the wrong things? What do you learn from his example?

3. Is God your treasure? How can you find more satisfaction in Him? Meditate on this passage and write down whatever God reveals to you.

"Don't store up treasures here on earth, where moths eat them and rust destroys them, and where thieves break in and steal. Store your treasures in heaven, where moths and rust cannot destroy, and thieves do not break in and steal. Wherever your treasure is, there the desires of your heart will also be." Mt. 6:19-21 NLT

Find the Freedom to Change

1. How did Zacchaeus respond after spending time with Jesus? How have you responded after spending time with Jesus as you have worked through this guide?

2. Read Luke 19:8-9 and 2 Cor. 5:17. Zacchaeus's attitude and values shift dramatically after spending time with Jesus. How did Zacchaeus's behavior change?

3. Name an attitude God has changed within you. How has this change affected what you value and how you behave?

Go in a New Direction!

1. Read Acts 9:1-22. How did an encounter with Jesus change the direction of Saul's life? What did this encounter inspire Saul (who later became the Apostle Paul) to do?

2. Has encountering Jesus changed the direction of your life? If so, write a brief description of how your direction (desires, plans, etc.) has changed.

3. What has the Lord inspired you to do? Write about something God has called you to do (it can be something big or small). What are your goals regarding this call?

ZACCHAEUS

What Do You Think?

"The kingdom of heaven is like treasure hidden in a field. When a man found it, he hid it again, and then in his joy went and sold all he had and bought that field."
Matt. 13:44

1. How is the story of Zacchaeus similar to the parable of the Hidden Treasure? How is it similar to your story?

2. Discuss with a friend how other people in your church have pursued Christ and His kingdom. What can you learn from them?

3. Find another biblical example of someone who sought after God (beyond the characters in this guide). What do you learn from his or her experience?

4. Discuss with a friend what the Lord has called you to do in His kingdom.

5. Journal and discuss something you have learned during this 40-day time of seeking God.

David

"Each time you worship, whether publicly or privately, dedicate the time to seeking God. Tell Him you are coming to see Him. Anticipate the joy of meeting Him. Engage your five senses. Loosen up and let go. God's people are leaping and singing, even now, in the spiritual realm. Let's join the celebration!"

Seeking a Familiar Face, PAGE 99

Rediscover the Joy of Worship

Read 1 Chron. 15:28-16:36 along with "David Seeks"
in *Seeking a Familiar Face*, pages 88-90.

· ❈ ·

1. Why do you think David danced as he worshipped with his people? List several possible reasons.

2. Do you find it difficult to enjoy worship like David did? If so, why? What inspires you (in the passage above) to worship more joyfully?

3. Select a verse from 1 Chron. 16:8-36 to use as a theme for your worship this week. Write the verse below. Prepare your heart before you worship by reading and praying over it several times.

Engage Mind, Body and Soul

Meditate on the following verses:

"Give praise to the Lord, proclaim his name; make known among the nations what he has done. Sing to him, sing praise to him; tell of all his wonderful acts. Glory in his holy name; let the hearts of those who seek the Lord rejoice. Look to the Lord and his strength; seek his face always." **Ps. 105:1-4**

1. Describe your most meaningful time of worship. How could you recapture that same feeling or experience?

2. *"Ezra praised the Lord, the great God; and all the people lifted their hands and responded, 'Amen! Amen!' Then they bowed down and worshiped the Lord with their faces to the ground."* Neh. 8:6

    How could you better engage your entire being in worship (mind, body and soul)?

3. Read John 4:23-24. What does worshipping God in "spirit and in truth" mean to you? Write a prayer asking God to help you worship sincerely from the heart. Ask Him to help you overcome any obstacles that might stand in your way.

Celebrate Worship with Others

1. Read Luke 22:7-34. In verse 15, Jesus said, *"I have **eagerly** desired to eat this Passover with you before I suffer."* Why do you think Jesus was eager to share the worship at the Passover feast with the disciples?

2. Are you eager to worship with other believers? How could you increase your joy and fulfillment while you worship with others?

3. List some of the blessings of belonging to the family of God. What do believers have in common? What can we celebrate together? How can worshipping with God's family encourage you?

Join the Heavenly Celebration!

1. Read Heb. 12:18-29. In this passage, Sinai, the mountain of fear (which the Israelites approached) is contrasted with Zion, the mountain of joy (which believers now approach). How does this passage paint a larger, more joyous picture of worship?

2. Read Rev. 19:1-7. What words in this passage describe the celebratory worship in heaven? What emotions do the heavenly worshipers display? Do you feel these same emotions when you worship? Why or why not?

3. How do these passages enlarge your understanding of worship? How can you connect your worship to the ongoing heavenly celebration?

1. Journal about what makes worship joyful to you. (Hint: find ideas from Psalms of worship such as Ps. 150, 95 or 66.) Discuss this with a friend.

2. What can you do when you don't feel like worshipping? Make a simple plan to help you overcome this feeling. (Hint: the titles within this chapter may provide ideas)

3. Journal about specific ways you can involve your mind, body and soul in worship. How can you keep worship "fresh" by changing it from time to time? Discuss this with a friend.

4. What obstacles can make group worship difficult? Journal about how you can overcome these obstacles.

5. Discuss with a friend what worshipping in "spirit and in truth" (John 4:23) means. What challenges you about worshipping this way?

Elijah

"WE TEND TO FORGET THAT EACH PRAYER
IS ETERNAL AND PRECIOUS. NOT ONE
PRAYER IS WASTED. NOT ONE PRAYER IS
FORGOTTEN."

SEEKING A FAMILIAR FACE, PAGE 114

Pray Through the Wait

Read 1 Kings 18:20-45 along with "Elijah Seeks"
in *Seeking a Familiar Face*, pages 104-106.

1. God answered Elijah's prayer immediately with fire from heaven. Describe a time when God answered one of your prayers quickly and powerfully.

2. Elijah repeated his prayer for rain seven times before he received an answer. What prayers are you waiting for God to answer right now?

3. Why do you think God made Elijah wait for an answer to his prayer for rain? Why might God make you wait for answers?

Pray Humbly Before God's Throne

1. In 1 Kings 18:42, Elijah knelt down and put his face between his knees as he prayed. How might kneeling have affected Elijah's attitude toward God?

2. How does kneeling in prayer affect your attitude toward God? Do you think you should kneel more often? Why or why not?

3. Elijah's humility before God was reflected in his posture and in his words of praise (1 Kings 18:36-37). What did this teach the Israelites? What does it teach you? What words of praise do you use as you pray?

Pray Directly for Answers

1. Elijah prayed directly, saying, *"Answer me Lord, answer me."* Write out a specific, detailed prayer list for today.

2. Read Hezekiah's prayer in 2 Kings 19:14-19. How was Hezekiah's prayer focused and direct? Is it difficult for you to pray this way? Why or Why not?

3. Even though Paul assures us that God can do immeasurably more than we ask or imagine (Eph. 3:20), do you ever feel like you are asking God for too much? Is it possible to ask God for too much?

Pray Persistently. Don't Give Up!

1. What inspires you to keep on praying even when God is silent? Find a few verses to support your answer.

2. Read Luke 18:1-8. What is the Lord teaching you right now about His silence? Is He encouraging you to be more persistent in prayer?

3. How might praying persistently grow your faith? How could praying this way change your perspective of people and events?

ELIJAH

1. Find a biblical example of someone who prayed with humility, directness or persistence. Journal about what you learn and then discuss it with a friend.

2. Do you ever feel awkward praying in front of others? If so, how could you overcome this feeling? Discuss your thoughts with a friend.

3. Find several verses about the blessings of praying with someone else.

4. List several reasons why writing your prayers in a journal might be beneficial.

5. Journal about how one of your prayers has been answered during this 40-day time of seeking God. Share your experience with a friend.

Ruth

"GOD WANTS TO HELP US LOVE ONE
ANOTHER. SEEK HIM. CONNECT WITH
HIS POWER. THIS WILL CHANGE EVERY
RELATIONSHIP YOU HAVE BECAUSE IT WILL
CHANGE YOU."

SEEKING A FAMILIAR FACE, PAGE 132

Love Your Inner Circle Well

Read Ruth 1-4, along with "Ruth Seeks"
in *Seeking a Familiar Face*, pages 120-123.

1. List the ways Ruth showed love to Naomi.

2. List the people in your inner circle (or those to whom you are close). Write an "H" by the names of those who are hard to love. Write an "E" by the names of those who are easy. And write "I" by the names of those who fall somewhere in-between.

3. Pray over your inner circle. Keep them in mind as you work through this chapter. How does the beautiful relationship between Ruth and Naomi inspire you to love those on your list more deeply?

Love Physically

Meditate on the following verses:

"This is how we know what love is: Jesus Christ laid down his life for us. And we ought to lay down our lives for our brothers and sisters. If anyone has material possessions and sees a brother or sister in need but has no pity on them, how can the love of God be in that person? Dear children, let us not love with words or speech but with actions and in truth." 1 John 3:16-18

1. List several ways Jesus displayed His love by caring for the physical needs of those who were closest to Him. (See John 6:10-15; 9:6-8; 11)

2. Think about the people who are on your inner circle list from day 1. How are you caring for their physical needs?

3. Certainly, you can't meet every physical need, but what needs can you meet for your inner circle? Write a prayer asking God to help you display love in tangible ways.

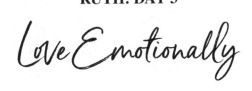

1. How did Ruth and Naomi meet the following emotional needs for each other?

    Acceptance:

    Gratitude:

    Encouragement:

    Respect:

    Blessing:

    Forgiveness:

2. How could you meet the same emotional needs for those in your inner circle?

    Acceptance:

    Gratitude:

    Encouragement:

    Respect:

    Blessing:

    Forgiveness:

3. Although you can't meet every emotional need of your inner circle, ask the Lord to help you meet their needs in a loving way. Write this prayer in the space below.

Love Spiritually

1. How did Ruth and Naomi care for each other on a spiritual basis?

2. One way to love someone spiritually is by praying for his or her faith. List what Paul prayed for the Colossian believers in Col. 1:9-12.

3. Are you praying for the faith of those in your inner circle? If not, why not? Mark one day a month on your calendar with a reminder to pray for your loved ones. Pray for their spiritual growth, strength and protection.

1. How does seeking the Lord affect our relationships? (See 1 John 4:7-12)

2. The way you love your inner circle is important to God (Mt. 22:36-40). Journal about how your love for God affects your love for your:

   a. Spouse

   b. Children

   c. Friends

   d. Church

3. Journal about how others have met your physical, emotional, and spiritual needs. Write a thank you note to someone in your inner circle who has loved you well.

4. Which emotional needs (listed on Day 3) are the most difficult for you to meet? Which needs are the easiest? Discuss your thoughts with a friend.

5. Does loving others spiritually make you uncomfortable? Discuss the best ways to love others in a spiritual sense.

Hannah

"GOD HAS MUCH GREATER PLANS IN MIND
FOR OUR LIVES THAN WE DO."

SEEKING A FAMILIAR FACE, PAGE 137

HANNAH: DAY 1

Surrender Even When You Don't Understand

Read 1 Samuel 1 along with "Hannah Seeks"
in *Seeking a Familiar Face*, pages 137-139.

1. After Hannah let go of her plan and surrendered to God's plan *for* her, she found peace. Have you ever experienced the peace of surrender? If so, when?

2. What is your greatest disappointment right now? Has this chipped away at your faith? Is your hope diminishing? If so, write a prayer telling God how you feel.

3. Hannah surrendered to God's purpose, even though she didn't understand it. How could you surrender your current problems to God's purpose? What changes might surrender bring?

God Sees You. Do You See Him?

1. When we are suffering, it's tempting to think that God doesn't see us or care about what happens to us. Find three verses that promise God sees and cares for us.

2. Have you become more aware of God's presence during this 40-day time of seeking? How can you train your eyes to see God in everyday situations?

3. Read Ps. 139:14-16. How has God watched over you in the past? How do you see Him working on your behalf now?

Surrender to Life as It Is Today

"We can rejoice, too, when we run into problems and trials, for we know that they are good for us—they help us learn to be patient. And patience develops strength of character in us and helps us trust God more each time we use it until finally our hope and faith are strong and steady. Then, when that happens, we are able to hold our heads high no matter what happens and know that all is well, for we know how dearly God loves us, and we feel this warm love everywhere within us because God has given us the Holy Spirit to fill our hearts with his love." Rom. 5:3-5 TLB

1. What circumstances are you struggling to accept right now? Write a prayer, using words and phrases from the passage above, asking God to help you surrender to your life as it is today, (instead of how you wish it would be).

2. According to the passage above, why is surrendering to God's will valuable? List the blessings that problems and trials can produce.

3. How could accepting your current circumstances possibly change your future circumstances?

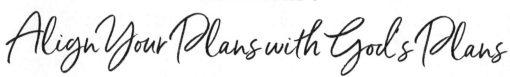

1. Describe a time when you had to change your plans to align with God's will. What did you learn?

2. Reread 1 Sam. 1. How did Hannah dedicate her dream (of having a son) to God? How can you dedicate your future plans and dreams to God for your:

   Marriage:

   Children:

   Career:

3. As you struggle to align your will with God's will, have you ever had a "Peninnah" to ridicule you or an "Eli" to misjudge you, like Hannah did? How did Hannah handle it? How have you handled it?

HANNAH

1. What circumstances are you struggling to accept right now, with your:

   a. Family

   b. Friends

   c. Work

   d. Church

2. Pray through the list above. How do you feel God calling you to surrender? Discuss what you learn with a friend.

3. Read Matt. 16:21-25. How did Peter struggle to surrender to God's plan? What future plans do you need to surrender to God?

4. How did seeking God change Hannah's future? Discuss with a friend how seeking God in surrender might change your life.

Barnabas

"The more we seek God, the more we discover about ourselves. In His presence, hidden gifts seem to bubble up from the depths of our soul. Opportunities to develop our talents are revealed. New resources come to light. Few things can bring us closer to God than following His call on our gifts."

Seeking a Familiar Face, PAGE 153

BARNABAS: DAY 1

Partner with God to Serve

**Read Acts 4:34-37, 9:26-28, 11:23-30 along with "Barnabas Seeks"
in *Seeking a Familiar Face*, pages 150-152.**

**As we seek God, gifts—in the form of talents and resources—seem to emerge,
as if God is inviting us to use them in partnership with Him.**

1. List some of the things Barnabas did to serve others.

2. How does his example challenge you today? How does it inspire you?

3. How did serving draw Barnabas closer to the Lord? Has serving done the same for you?
    Why or why not?

Discover Your Gifts & Resources

The more we seek God, the more we discover about ourselves.

Meditate on the following verses:

"Each person is given something to do that shows who God is . . ." 1 Cor. 12:7 MSG

"God has given each of you a gift from his great variety of spiritual gifts. Use them well to serve one another." 1 Peter 4:10 NLT

"Work for the things that make peace and help each other become stronger Christians." Rom 14:19 NLV

1. List your personal gifts, strengths, and talents.

2. How could you use your gifts, strengths, and talents to serve others? Brainstorm in the space below.

3. List personal resources, such as a car or house, education, relationships, or past experiences. How could you use these things to serve others? Brainstorm in the space below.

Discover the Connection

Meditate on the following verse:

"To those who use well what they have been given, even more will be given, and they will have an abundance. But from those who do nothing, even what little they have will be taken away." Matt. 25:29 NLT

Few things can bring us closer to God than following His call on our gifts. And when we use all that we have to glorify Him, it draws us even closer.

1. Examine your lists of gifts and resources (from Day 2) closely. Are you using what you have been given well? How could you glorify God with your gifts and resources?

2. Do you see a connection between your gifts and resources? Could they somehow be used together for a specific purpose?

3. Write a prayer thanking God for what He has given you. Ask Him to help you use your gifts to serve Him today.

Discover Opportunities to Serve

Meditate on the following verse:

"Do not neglect to do good and to share what you have, for such sacrifices are pleasing to God." Heb. 13:16 ESV

As we seek God, He often points out the needs of others to us, like He did for Barnabas. When God reveals a need, He is inviting us to use our gifts to meet it.

1. Have opportunities to serve others emerged as you have spent time with God during these 40 days? If so, how have you met these opportunities?

2. Does using your gifts make you feel closer to God? Why or why not?

3. Make a list of future areas of service you would like to pursue. Pray over this list and write down any guidance that you receive.

BARNABAS

1. Reread Acts 4:34-37, 9:26-28, 11:23-30. How did Barnabas discover his gift of encouragement? How can you help someone else discover their gifts? Brainstorm with a friend.

2. How did Barnabas use his gift of encouragement to bless others?

3. Name and discuss various gifts and resources that could have a spiritual use.

4. Do you know your calling (or at least part of it)? If so, describe it in the space below and share how God revealed it to you with a friend.

5. Journal about recent opportunities you have had to serve others. How did serving make you feel? Did it open up doors to new areas of service? What opportunities to serve would you like to have in the future?

Guided Meditations

"I WILL REMEMBER THE DEEDS OF THE LORD; YES, I
WILL REMEMBER YOUR WONDERS OF OLD.
I WILL PONDER ALL YOUR WORK, AND MEDITATE ON
YOUR MIGHTY DEEDS."

Ps. 77:11-12 ESV

MEDITATION 1

When You Need Rest

Jesus calls weary souls to come to Him for rest. The kind of rest that Jesus gives is far better than a vacation can give. No special mattress or sleeping pill can offer soul-rest like Jesus offers. Today, meditate on entering into that state of rest. Feel refreshed, as if your soul has found a shady oasis in the middle of a hot, dry desert.

Prepare your heart for this meditation by reading these verses aloud:

"Are you weary, carrying a heavy burden? Then come to me. I will refresh your life, for I am your oasis. Simply join your life with mine. Learn my ways and you'll discover that I'm gentle, humble, easy to please. You will find refreshment and rest in me. For all that I require of you will be pleasant and easy to bear." Mt. 11:28-30 TPT

Breathe deeply several times. Each time you exhale, try to relax your body and clear your mind. Sit in a comfortable position. Close your eyes or focus them on this meditation.

MINUTE 1:
I Rest in You.

Be completely still for one minute. Relax your body and your mind. Then rest your soul:

Rest from trying to save yourself—you can't.

Rest from trying to be worthy of salvation—you aren't.

Rest from trying to justify yourself—you can't.

Just as God rested after creation was finished, so now you can rest in Christ's finished work. No matter what happens today, your soul is safe and your future is secure, not because of what you've done, but because of what He did for you.

If your mind wanders, gently bring it back by saying, "I rest in you."

MINUTE 2:
I Enjoy Your Rest.

Picture yourself as a weary traveler who has entered into God's rest (Heb. 4:9-11). He is the oasis for your soul. Drink in His living water. Rest in the shadow of His wings. Enjoy this minute of peace in your body, mind, and soul. Don't let distractions steal it away. Delight in God's rest and refreshment; carry them with you throughout the day.

If your mind wanders, gently bring it back by saying, "I enjoy your rest."

When You Need Strength

When we encounter God, we encounter the most powerful being there is. No one can defeat Him. Nothing can stand against Him. As you come before God Almighty today, feel His strength and power. Be still and know it. Let Him strengthen you.

Read these verses a few times out loud to prepare your heart for this meditation:

"It is God who arms me with strength and makes my way perfect." Ps. 18:32 NKJV

"But the Lord stood at my side and gave me strength, so that through me the message might be fully proclaimed . . ." 2 Tim. 4:17

"My grace is all you need. My power works best in weakness." 2 Cor. 12:9 NLT

Breathe deeply several times. Each time you exhale, try to relax your body and clear your mind. Sit in a comfortable position. Close your eyes or focus them on this meditation.

MINUTE 1:
You are strong.

For one minute, meditate on God's power:

He is powerful in word.

Mighty in every deed.

Strong a thousand years ago, strong now and forever.

Feel His powerful presence within you. Lift your hands in recognition of His strength.

If your mind wanders, gently bring it back again by saying, "You are strong."

MINUTE 2:
Strengthen me.

For one minute, receive God's strength. Imagine it flowing down like anointing oil. Accept it gratefully, humbly. Focus on how receiving a measure of God's great strength makes you feel. Remember, the Lord lends you strength so that you can glorify Him. Use His strength to serve and to love others well. Live strong. Let God empower you to do great things in His kingdom today.

If your mind wanders, gently bring it back again by saying, "Strengthen me."

When You Are Down

Moses was one of the greatest spiritual leaders in the Bible, yet at Mt. Sinai, his people strayed away from God and worshipped a golden calf. After this, Moses must have felt pretty low. But instead of focusing on how he felt, he asked to see God's glory. God revealed His glory to Moses (Ex. 33:18-23). This amazing encounter pulled Moses out of despair and inspired him on to victory. God's glory can do the same for us.

Read these verses out loud a few times to prepare your heart for this meditation:

"If then you have been raised with Christ, seek the things that are above, where Christ is, seated at the right hand of God. Set your minds on things that are above, not on things that are on earth." Col. 3:1-2 ESV

"But we all, seeing the glory of the Lord with unveiled faces, as in a mirror, are being transformed into the same image from glory to glory by the Spirit of the Lord." 2 Cor. 3:18 MEV

Breathe deeply several times. Each time you exhale, try to relax your body and clear your mind. Sit in a comfortable position. Close your eyes or focus them on this meditation.

MINUTE 1:
Show me your glory.

For one minute, consciously shift your mind's gaze away from problems and busyness toward God. Consider these aspects of His glory:

He is the loving Creator.
>He is always good.

He is a magnificent Savior.
>He is perfectly just.

He is a glorious Father.
>He is a promise keeper.

Ask God to reveal His glory to you. Experience it and celebrate it.

If your mind wanders, gently bring it back again by saying, "Show me your glory."

MINUTE 2:
Help me reflect your glory.

For one minute, imagine yourself standing in a radiant shaft of light, lifting a giant mirror above your head. Adjust the mirror to reflect the bright light toward those you love. Watch as the light touches them. Take note of its brilliance, beauty and power. This is what happens when we glorify God—we reflect His light. Let His glory shine forth in your words and deeds, today.

If your mind wanders, gently bring it back again by saying out loud, "Help me reflect your glory."

When You Need Grace

The Lord invites us to come before His throne to receive mercy and grace whenever we need it. It's one of the most beautiful invitations we will ever receive and one we should not take lightly. As you meditate before the throne of God today, ask Him to supply the grace you need.

Read this verse a few times out loud to prepare your heart for meditation:

> *"So let us keep on coming boldly to the throne of grace, so that we may obtain mercy and find grace to help us in our time of need." Heb. 4:16 ISV*

Breathe deeply several times. Each time you exhale, try to relax your body and clear your mind. Sit in a comfortable position. Close your eyes or focus them on this meditation.

MINUTE 1:
Receive grace.

For one minute, picture yourself kneeling before God's throne of grace. You've been invited here, so come boldly, reverently. Ask the Lord to forgive your sins. Confess, repent and be washed as white as snow. Now, forgive yourself. Release any lingering feelings of guilt. Delight in how it feels to be holy, clean, and pure, for there is no longer any "condemnation (or guilt) to those who are in Christ Jesus." (Rom. 8:1).

If your mind wanders, gently bring it back again by saying, "I receive your grace."

MINUTE 2:
Let grace overflow.

As you kneel before God's throne, imagine grace flowing from it like a raging river. Let it wash over you, saturating your mind, soul and body. Feel this "Niagara" of grace set you free. Let it overflow. God no longer holds your sins against you; release whatever you hold against someone else. Forgive. Let grace flow mightily through you today.

If your mind wanders, gently bring it back again by saying, "Let grace overflow."

MEDITATION 5

When You Are Down

Disappointment, loneliness and grief can weigh us down, dominate our thoughts and even affect our behavior. But we can choose to release these heavy feelings to God. Ps. 55:22 says, "Give your burdens to the Lord, and he will take care of you." As you meditate, choose to let go of your troubled feelings for just a few minutes. Give your mind needed rest. Make mental "room" to receive God's love.

Read these verses out loud a few times to prepare your heart for this meditation:

"Give all your worries and cares to God, for he cares about you." 1 Pet. 5:7 NLT

"The steadfast love of the Lord never ceases; his mercies never come to an end; they are new every morning; great is your faithfulness. 'The Lord is my portion,' says my soul, 'therefore I will hope in him.' The Lord is good to those who wait for him, to the soul who seeks him." Lam. 3:22-25 ESV

Breathe deeply several times. Each time you exhale, try to relax your body and clear your mind. Sit in a comfortable position. Close your eyes or focus them on this meditation.

MINUTE 1:
Release your pain.

Are you frustrated? Give your frustration to God. Are you angry? Release your anger—and whatever your anger stems from—up to Him. Let go of heavy feelings such as sorrow, inadequacy and rejection. Watch them rise, as if they were in a balloon floating up and away. Releasing your pain makes mental "room" for you to receive God's love. Being in God's presence, even for just a minute, makes you feel much brighter and lighter than before.

If your mind wanders, gently bring it back by saying, "I release my pain."

MINUTE 2:
Receive love.

For the second minute, open your hands to receive God's love. His love for you is unlimited and unchanging. It endures forever. Think about it: an ocean of love, blessing, joy, and hope is available to you. Receive it. Store it away in the empty places of your heart. God's love will help you face whatever happens today.

If your mind wanders, gently bring it back by saying, "I receive your love."

When You're Facing a Trial

When we face trials, we often experience spiritual "amnesia," losing sight of God's past provision and protection. The Bible reminds us of what the Lord has already done so that we will trust in Him today. If you are going through a trial right now, think about how God helped you in the past. Expect His help again, for He does not change.

Read these verses a few times out loud to prepare your heart for this meditation:

"I remember the days of long ago; I meditate on all your works and consider what your hands have done." Ps. 143:5

"Remember the things I have done in the past. For I alone am God! I am God, and there is none like me." Isa. 46:9 NLT

Breathe deeply several times. Each time you exhale, try to relax your body and clear your mind. Sit in a comfortable position. Close your eyes or focus them on this meditation.

MINUTE 1:
I remember your wonders.

For one minute, remember the wonders of creation. Picture one of the most beautiful places you have ever been. Go back there mentally. Experience it again. Look at the natural beauty. Hear the sounds. Enjoy the wonder of what He has made.

If your mind wanders, gently bring it back by saying, "I remember your wonders."

MINUTE 2:
I remember your promises.

For the second minute, focus on the beautiful promises of God. Here's a list to inspire you:

God has given me eternal life through Christ. (1 John 5:11)

God's grace abounds to me; He will meet my needs. (2 Corinthians 9:8)

I am being transformed into His likeness each day. (2 Corinthians 3:18)

My future inheritance will never perish, spoil, or fade. (1 Peter 1:3-4)

No one can ever separate me from the love of Christ. (Romans 8:35-39)

Your trial will not last forever, but God's promises will. Remember to Whom you belong. If God is for you, who can be against you? (Rom. 8:31) Practice remembering this throughout the day.

If your mind wanders, gently bring it back by saying, "I remember your promises."

When You Need Joy

In Psalm 104, the psalmist takes us through a four-part meditation centered on rejoicing in the Lord. Let's follow along!

Breathe deeply several times. Each time you exhale, try to relax your body and clear your mind. Sit in a comfortable position.

MINUTE 1:
You are majestic.

Read Ps. 104:1-4. For one minute, close your eyes and focus on God's majesty. These verses paint a beautiful picture: God is robed in honor and splendor; He is wrapped in light. He makes the clouds His chariot and rides on the wings of the wind.

If your mind wanders, gently bring it back by saying, "You are majestic."

MINUTE 2:
You are the Creator.

Read Ps. 104:5-23. For one minute, close your eyes and focus on God the Creator. Imagine God setting the earth in place and covering it with land and water. Next He sets the sun and moon in place to regulate time and seasons. Then He spins the globe and sets creation into motion, beginning the cycle of life upon the earth. His creation is intricate and wonderful.

If your mind wanders, gently bring it back by saying, "You are my Creator."

MINUTE 3:
You are the sustainer of life.

Read Ps. 104:24-30. For one minute, imagine God opening His hand to feed all of His creatures, both big and small. Each one is richly satisfied. Now picture Him opening His hand wide toward you to satisfy your needs. Feel His concern and care over you.

If your mind wanders, gently bring it back by saying, "You are my sustainer."

MINUTE 4:
I rejoice in You.

Read Ps. 104:31-35. For one minute, rejoice in the Lord. Give Him glory, honor, and praise. Tell Him you love Him now and always. Smile. Thank Him for all He has done for you.

If your mind wanders, gently bring it back by saying, "I rejoice in you, Lord."

About the Author

May Patterson, author of the book *Seeking a Familiar Face* and its companion Bible study, *A 40-Day Guide for Seeking God* began writing in response to God's grace. And by His grace, she has written articles for magazines such as *Focus on the Family, Crosswalk* and *The Upper Room,* and is a sought-after public speaker. She loves to tell stories, laugh, and talk about the incredible journey of seeking after God.

May feels blessed to have lived in Huntsville, Alabama all of her life. She is married to her dear friend Mike and they have three grown children. When she is not writing or speaking, you might find her on a hiking trail, riding a horse, or even aboard an airplane traveling to somewhere new. She has a great love for family, outdoor adventures, books and blogging.

CONNECT WITH MAY:

Blog maypatterson.com.

facebook.com/May.Patterson.7

may.patterson

hello_patterson

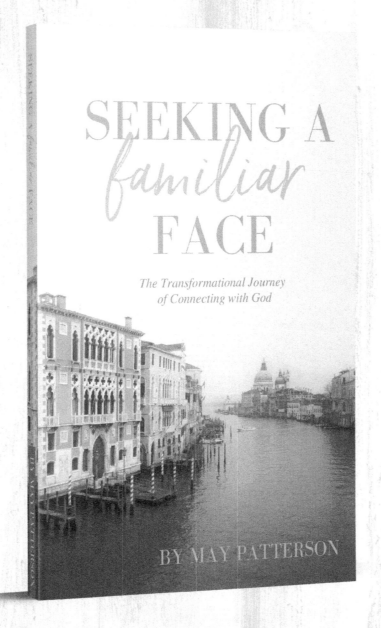

Made in the USA
Coppell, TX
20 February 2020

16020482R00044